MURPHY'S LAWS
of bridge

Joe Blatnick

authorHOUSE®

AuthorHouse™
1663 Liberty Drive
Bloomington, IN 47403
www.authorhouse.com
Phone: 1 (800) 839-8640

Published by AuthorHouse 12/18/2015

ISBN: 978-1-5049-4822-7 (sc)
ISBN: 978-1-5049-4823-4 (e)

Print information available on the last page.

This book is printed on acid-free paper.

Introduction

Legend has it that our fate lies in the hands of a mysterious and far from benevolent character called Murphy. No one seems to know which of life's endeavours spawned this negative individual but the laws attributed to Murphy can be applied, without hesitation, to any of them. Simply stated, this law says, "ANYTHING THAT CAN GO WRONG, WILL". And Bridge, with its myriad of possible hands which can be dealt, bids which can be made, Declarer play techniques from which to choose and countless defensive strategies which can be followed, lends itself to Murphy's Law in more ways than can be imagined.

I like to say that my luck is so bad that when my ship finally comes in, I'll be at the airport.

But is it really bad luck or just another normal day at the office for Murphy. As you read through the over two hundred perverse applications of Murphy's Law to Bridge, you be the judge - luck, fate or Murphy at his diabolical best.

You'll recognize the zany results which you thought only happened to you and instead of blaming your partner for those bad scores, you'll finally realize who the real culprit is and place the blame where it truly belongs.

Joe

PHILOSOPHICAL

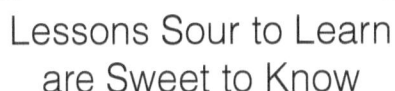

Lessons Sour to Learn
are Sweet to Know

Someone suggested that I smile,
trump could have broken 5 - 1. So
I smiled and sure as night follows
day, on the next hand, they did.

The Bridge gods can only help
one player per hand. This hand
is certainly not your turn and the
next one doesn't look to be either.

If you outthink yourself in Bridge,
it's called '*Paralysis by Analysis*'.

Confidence disappears as soon
as dummy hits the table.

The six stages of Bridge are *'Know Little'*, followed by *'Frenzied Learning'* and then *'Complete Frustration'*. These are followed by *'Some Improvement'*, *'Brief Satisfaction'* and *'Complete Frustration'*.

You can duplicate the same winning formula on the next hand by simply throwing your cards in the air.

Just when you think partner has forgiven your last blunder, you commit a beaut.

Set realistic goals and you won't be disappointed. 40% seems about right.

Just when you think you're ready for the big leagues the wheels fall off.

If you think you played badly today, wait till the next game.

You think you've got a handle on that technique. Then it comes up for real.

Playing really badly will occur when you are trying to impress a former student.

Some players go into the tank. Others simply fall asleep.

When others tell you that your game only needs a little tweaking, they haven't grasped the situation.

Look on the bright side - you haven't lost a match, you've found a reason to come back for more abuse.

It's always partner's fault.

The other technique is always best, unless it's the other one.

Fool me once, shame on you; fool me twice, shame on me; fool me thrice and I'm a bridge player.

There is no limit on bad hands because the law of averages only works for others.

A true bridge expert has the ability to avoid all those little mistakes and proceed directly to a major blunder.

With some bridge players, genius is gone in a flash while stupidity lingers.

For a player to do something really foolish, incompetence is not enough, it needs to be seen by many.

An unsolicited lesson is about as welcome as drawing the village idiot for a partner.

Slams are easy to make, just sign off in game.

The person whom you dragged to the club wins and suddenly wants to play every day.

Everyone has the strength of character to misplay a cold slam.

If a director has to play, he'll get numerous calls, but very few if he isn't.

The only truly annoying characteristic of a bridge partner, is the ability to win every post mortem.

Suits will break proportionately to how badly you need them to.

You never run out of bad hands.

The perfect hand is the one you have just dealt and passed down two tables.

To some, Bridge is a few hours of feeling incompetent, punctuated by a few moments of sheer boredom.

Never let the slow player know that you're in a hurry.

If it ain't broke, you ain't tried it yet.

Things you learn are temporary and improvement never lasts.

Never ask a bridge teacher if you should take lessons.

There are two secrets to winning bridge and I can't remember either.

AIN'T IT THE TRUTH

The Bridge Gods are Always in the Other Guy's Corner

Getting a top score on a difficult hand, late in the game, is much easier if you're playing at a 30% clip.

Bridge is not life or death. It's much more important than that.

Every Bridge hand matches your ability against your opponent's luck.

A Law of Bridge:
Every good decision is accompanied by a bad one.

When there is no hope of winning, is when your game will suddenly improve.

The reason that it's called Bridge is that, in many cases you're on a bridge to nowhere.

Bridge is a difficult game because 1/2 is bidding, 1/2 is Declarer play and 1/2 is defence.

In a play through, your second half will go badly if you could have coasted to victory.

The easiest way to find that favourite Bridge book which you misplaced is to buy a new one.

After a hand has left your table is when you realize how it could have been made.

Bad splits come in bunches, good ones individually.

We keep making the same mistakes because the only thing we learn from experience is that we learn nothing from experience.

If it wasn't for bridge, we'd have to fight with total strangers.

TOO LATE

Post Mortems Should be
Kept to a Minimum
and Criticism Taboo.
Both are Futile.

Experience: Recognizing a mistake when you make it again.

If your play always improves as a session progresses, next time start with the last hand.

It's usually about 3 hands later when you realize what you should have done on that disastrous hand.

BE REALISTIC

When Both Opponents
Discard, all Trump Have
Been Drawn.

Bridge players who claim not to look at opponent's cards are also liars.

You won't feel fulfilled until you've learned the '*Idaho Transfer*' - transfer the blame to partner.

The director isn't always watching. You decide whether or not you're entitled to a peek.

If you think you can't, you're probably right.

She is so accustomed to having her own way, she fills out her convention card in advance.

All's fair in love, war & Bridge.

There is a very simple way to improve your Bridge score - an eraser.

A peek isn't cheating unless you're caught.

DECISIONS

When You Decide to Play
for the Drop is When You
Should Have Finessed.

Two chances are better than one
for everyone but you.

The law of averages is never on
your side.

No matter how long you agonize,
you still have to play a card.

When faced with a difficult
decision, ask yourself what Goren
would have done and then don't
do it. It'll never work for you.

The reason that good play
is expensive in terms of time
and effort, is that it includes a
complimentary case of blunders.

You're probably right if you think
you're doing something wrong.

Your worst choice would have
been your best.

The most difficult hands are the
easy ones.

RESULTS

You Must Accept the Fact
that Some Days You're
the Bug and Some Days
the Windshield.

Bad results always pile up faster
than they can be forgotten.

If you can smile after a bad result,
you've probably won the post
mortem.

Your game hasn't really bottomed
out until you can't find a partner.

Just when you put that bad result
behind you, someone mentions it
again.

A good loser is still a loser.

Some days, even with everything working, you're still one trick short. Other days one good result is a winning streak.

When a risky play succeeds, it was planned. When the same risky play fails, the Bridge gods are being unfair.

You feel reasonably satisfied with your second place finish until some wise guy points out that you're at the front of a long line of losers.

Playing against a strong pair you feel lost. Against a weak pair you also feel lost. You can't figure out what they're doing.

MISTAKES

Finding Someone on Whom
to Blame Yours, Shows
Management Potential.

Just as you begin to feel confident at the table, someone points out another one of your mistakes.

There doesn't seem to be any fixing your game. What you try today should have been tried yesterday or saved for tomorrow.

The boards couldn't have been shuffled. I'm making the same mistakes which I made yesterday.

It seems that the only thing that you learn from your mistakes is that you never learn from your mistakes.

Correcting a flaw in your game simply exposes others.

Everyone would like to play error free. But they would be appeased if you simply made a few more of your own.

You always fall victim to a memory coup.

Some days it's easier to solve all of man's problems than it is to play error free.

If you really want to master Bridge, give it up.

The percentage play works for everyone else.

TEACHING & LEARNING

The Difference Between Genius and Stupidity is that Genius has its Limits.

The knowledge of the teachers successor,
As years passed grew lesser and lesser.
It at last grew so small,
He knew nothing at all.
So now he's a bridge professor.

You can learn most aspects of
Bridge through constant repetition.
But try and recall them during a
game.

Presenting some players with an
opportunity for a phantom save, is
a sure-fire positive result. Sadly
it's still the best part of this author's
game.

You never remember what you learned in class when it comes up in a game.

The best thing to take from a lesson to a game is crib notes.

All your problems in this game can be traced to one guru or another.

Never teach your spouse, take lessons from or play with him or her.

There is no defence against bad Bridge.

You can't teach judgement and you can't learn luck.

PACE

All Hesitation Normally
Does is Prolong
the Inevitable.

You can't be accused of taking too much time if you're praying for help.

Play is always faster in the other section.

Nobody ever plays too quickly or too quietly.

It only takes a moment to hide the convention card left behind by the slow pair you are following.

No matter how hard you try to avoid them you always end up following the slowest pair.

Just when you're on a roll, the director is called to the table at which you play next, delaying the slow pair even more.

When you have no interest in a hand and would rather get on to the next one is exactly when Declarer will go into a lengthy trance.

TEAMS

No Matter How You Slice it,
There are Always Two Sides.

In a team-of-four match there will be at least one hand where you coulda, woulda, shoulda.

In any Swiss match, the chance of making a difficult contract is inversely proportional to the importance.

In a team game, good hands will not surface until the last match, unless, of course, it's when you replace a team mate.

The score turned in for a Swiss match should only be considered as an initial offer.

If you are able to avoid the two obnoxious loud mouths as pick-up partners, it's only because the partnership desk has the couple from hell waiting for you.

NOT EVERYTHING COMES IN THREES

There are 3 Distinct Parts to a Bridge Hand
- Bidding, Declarer Play, Defence & Post Mortem.

$1 + 2 = 4$

Bad things happen in threes only for the other guy, For you they come in packages of four or more.

The Four Horsemen of the Apocolypse

- The phantom save

- Playing game in a 4/3 fit

- Playing game in a minor when 4 is cold in N.T.

- A weak 3 opener having your missing honour

WAGERING

Yogi Berra is Supposed
to Have Said,
"A Nickel Ain't Worth
a Dime Anymore."

Two fools and their money should be at your table.

There's a good reason for checking the traveller.

It's always after making a bet that your opponent's entourage shows up.

If you want to make one less trick, bet on it.

There is no such thing as a friendly wager. It's dog eat dog.

As the amount wagered goes up, the chances of making your contract go down.

A fool and his money makes an excellent opponent.

The weak opponents are always some place else, unless you're some place else and then they're some place else.

Your peers will accept your story more readily if you omit the part about your genius.

BIDDING

When my Wife Began
Crawling Under the Table,
I Asked, "What are You
Doing, my Dear?" Her Reply,
"I'm Looking for the Cards
You've Been Bidding."

The best bid is the one you didn't make.

You bid on when partner was planning a penalty double.

You always try to be imaginative on the wrong hands.

You have a perfect Flannery but it's their bid.

Bridge is 75% bidding and 25% bidding.

Every time I make a lead - directing bid partner is void.

When I make a pre-emptive bid,
partner has a 2 Club opening.

The bad bid on this hand would
have been perfect on the last one.

You always find that you should
have accepted that bid out of turn.

It's easy to make 4 Hearts or 4
Spades - simply stop at 3.

The good hands switch to N/S
just as soon as you sit E/W.

You decide to play 3 N.T. with
4 - 3 - 3 - 3 distribution but 4 of
the major is better.

You are finally convinced that you should be doubling part scores and the first time you do, guess what happens?

You double because you have A/Q behind Declarer. Guess who has K/J/x?

You upgrade your hand because you have length in the suit bid by R.H.O. and guess who's void? Not partner.

You always seem to bid one level above or below what you can make.

You can hear a hand being discussed 3 or 4 tables away but you can't hear what partner called from dummy.

Nothing has a more negative effect on your play of a hand than to have bid it perfectly.

You only need an S.O.S. redouble if you are foolish enough to have made the bids which invite a penalty in the first place.

Your part score bids should have been game and your game bids should have been slams.

You should have made the other bid, unless it was the other one, in which case you should have made the other one.

With just a few more opportunities you could make every bad bid imaginable.

It's the right bid but you convince yourself that it's the wrong one. Overcalling with a raggedy-suit works for others.

That perfect bid which you were going to make is no longer possible because the opponents got in the way.

Just as soon as you make a bid, you'll discover another card, in your hand, which would have provided you with a better one.

The more you try to steer partner to a 3N.T. contract the more he'll opt for a major suit game on a 4/3 fit.

You only get a perfect Stayman or transfer hand when an opponent opens 1N.T.

You have a perfect 4 - 4 - 4 - 1 for a take-out double but your R.H.O. opens one of your 4 card suits.

Whenever I get a hand which would be a perfect Western cuebid, this partner plays Eastern.

When you make a take-out double holding two 4 card majors, partner always bids a minor.

When you've stretched your values during the bidding, guess who'll be dummy and can't hide?

The bidding is always perfect until you see the dummy.

You have the perfect distribution for a reverse but not enough points. And when points are right distribution isn't.

As soon as you decide to play Flannery (5 Hearts, 4 Spades, 11 - 15 pts.) you'll get a mini-Roman hand (three 4-card suits and a singleton, 11 - 15 pts.) Both are opened 2 Diamonds.

There are only two basic bidding systems - the one you know and the one you should.

When partner opens 2♣ and you have a weak hand with a long suit, guess who'll be void in it.

CONVENTIONS

Another Quote Attributed to Yogi Berra. After a Convention Led to Disaster, He Would Have Said, "We Made too Many Wrong Errors".

Obsolete: the convention which you finally learned.

The best thing about obscure conventions is that nobody will know when you misuse them.

As soon as you master a new convention, partner has discovered a better one.

When you decide not to play a convention because of infrequent opportunity, it presents itself on the next hand.

Useless conventions attract. Sensible agreements repel. Finessing prayers are never answered.

The more complex a convention, the more useless information it conveys.

Unusual conventions have a short life span.

Bad and/or useless conventions always attract those who don't know their basics.

Never adopt a new convention until you've had a chance to misuse it.

When I make a take-out double, partner always responds in my worst suit.

DECLARER PLAY

"This is Another Fine Mess
You've Gotten Me into,
Stanley".

- Oliver

When you have 2 finesses to take
you always choose the wrong
one.

> With a choice of two identical
> suits to develop, you should have
> chosen the other.

When there is nothing at stake
you'll play perfectly.

> All your finesses will succeed
> when you stop at 3 of the major.

Trying a 75% option for success
never works but the 25% would
have.

You always duck a trick to the wrong opponent.

All your finesses will fail when all you needed was one of them.

If you must have a top you'll misguess the finesse.

You never see the right play until it's too late.

Your finesses always lose to a stiff King.

Everyone sees you misplay an easy hand but nobody ever witnesses your devil's coup.

By not trying a safety play which is eminently correct, the other guy gets a better result.

That new technique which you've just learned will never come up until you've forgotten it.

A suit will never break 3/3 when your last card is a spot.

With a choice of two techniques, try the other one first.

Your suit establishment effort would have worked perfectly on the previous hand.

In the middle of plan 'A' it becomes obvious that you've chosen the wrong plan.

When I play 3N.T., 4 of the major would have been better and when I play 4 of the major, it loses to 3N.T. + one.

Everyone else makes the contract because they didn't get a trump lead.

With a choice between two lines of play, the best one will always be the other one

The time you apply the 'Eight Ever, Nine Never' guideline is the time you should have finessed.

Just when you learn the value of discarding losers on extra winners, you'll have nothing but mirrored suits.

Nobody will see you execute a double squeeze but the whole bridge community will be watching when you blow a cold slam.

The 3 finesses which you just lost in the play of this hand are the ones you should have tried on the previous one.

If your finesse doesn't work, try it on the previous hand.

Finesses will always work if you don't need them.

There once was a man from Vinesse,
Who thought success would be a finesse.
But the King proved to be wrong,
It was not where it belonged.
So instead of more, he got less.

You should have taken that finesse immediately, unless you did, in which case you should have taken it on the next round, but if you had, it would have been too soon, but it's really a moot point since you didn't have the right cards to try it in the first place.

The success of a finesse is directly proportional to how badly you need it.

DEFENCE

"A Player Who Can't Defend Properly, Should Try to Become Declarer".
- *Alfred Sheinwold*

That brilliant play of your dreams never seems to work when the chips are on the line.

A suit will always break 3/3 when you can't get to that 13th card.

OR

It'll break 3/3 when your last card is an Ace.

A superbly played hand will only occur in your imagination while one poorly played will be on vu-graph.

Given enough opportunities you can make most of the defensive blunders known to man.

When you desperately need a count signal, you'll be playing with a partner who never heard of them!

I'm passive when I should be aggressive, and aggressive when I should be passive.

It seems that the only one who benefits from your signals is Declarer.

The lead which you thought to be correct, would have been on this next hand.

When you hold 2 identical suits
- one a major and one a minor,
when leading against 3N.T., you
always lead the major except
when you should have led the
minor.

An insignificant lead out of turn
will cost you the chance to defeat
a game which has only been bid
at your table.

When you finally accept the
wisdom of not underleading an
Ace on the opening lead, is the
time when doing so would have
been the only winning strategy.